# REAL-LIFE VAMPIRES

# BLOODSUCKING
# FLEAS AND TICKS

BY CHRISTINE HONDERS

Gareth Stevens
PUBLISHING

Please visit our website, www.garethstevens.com. For a free color catalog of all our high-quality books, call toll free 1-800-542-2595 or fax 1-877-542-2596.

**Library of Congress Cataloging-in-Publication Data**

Honders, Christine, author.
 Bloodsucking fleas and ticks / Christine Honders.
     pages cm. — (Real-life vampires)
 Includes bibliographical references and index.
 ISBN 978-1-4824-3943-4 (pbk.)
 ISBN 978-1-4824-3944-1 (6 pack)
 ISBN 978-1-4824-3945-8 (library binding)
 1. Fleas—Juvenile literature. 2. Ticks—Juvenile literature. 3. Bloodsucking insects—Juvenile literature. I. Title.
 QL599.5.H66 2016
 595—dc23

                              2015031503

First Edition

Published in 2016 by
**Gareth Stevens Publishing**
111 East 14th Street, Suite 349
New York, NY 10003

Copyright © 2016 Gareth Stevens Publishing

Designer: Katelyn E. Reynolds
Editor: Kristen Nelson

Photo credits: Cover, p. 1 Erik Karits/Shutterstock.com; cover, pp. 1–24 (background art) happykanppy/Shutterstock.com; p. 5 (dog) Natee K Jindakum/Shutterstock.com; p. 5 (flea) Visuals Unlimited, Inc./Robert Pickett/Getty Images; p. 7 (tick) D. Kucharski K. Kucharska/ Shutterstock.com; p. 7 (flea) Alastair Macewen/Oxford Scientific/Getty Images; p. 9 UsagiP/ Shutterstock.com; p. 11 CLOUDS HILL IMAGING LTD/Science Photo Library/Getty Images; p. 13 Stephen Dalton/Minden Pictures/Getty Images; p. 15 Marcel Langelaan/Buiten-beeld/ Minden Pictures/Getty Images; p. 17 James Gathany/courtesy of the CDC; p. 19 Crystal Eye Studio/Shutterstock.com; p. 21 (illustrations) Dn Br/Shutterstock.com.

Printed in the United States of America

CPSIA compliance information: Batch #CW16GS: For further information contact Gareth Stevens, New York, New York at 1-800-542-2595.

# CONTENTS

Words in the glossary appear in **bold** type
the first time they are used in the text.

# VAMPIRE BUGS!

It's a warm summer day, and you see that your dog can't stop **scratching**. You reach over to pet him and see flat, reddish-brown bugs about the size of a pinhead running around in his fur. Your poor pooch has fleas. And they're not just biting him—they're drinking his blood!

Some bugs eat plants or other bugs. Fleas and ticks need to drink blood to live. They're tiny, real-life **vampires**!

FACT BITE

Fleas can make amazing jumps, more than 100 times the length of their body. That's how they get onto your pet!

# PARASITIC PESTS

Fleas and ticks are parasites, which are **organisms** that live on or in another organism. The organism a parasite lives on is called the host. A parasite needs a host for food, often eating parts of it. Without the host, the parasite would die. Some kinds of parasites cause their *hosts* to die, though.

There are many kinds of parasites. Endoparasites live inside their hosts. Fleas and ticks are ectoparasites, which means that they live on their host's skin.

FACT BITE

You can tell ticks and fleas apart easily because ticks have eight legs and fleas have six.

tick

flea

# A FLEA'S LIFE

The most common flea is the cat flea, which feasts on cats, dogs, and people. All fleas have the same four-part life cycle.

First, a flea lays eggs on a host. The eggs fall off it and **hatch** into larvae. Larvae live in dark, warm places like pet beds! After several days, the larvae spin cocoons and become pupae. Once an adult flea breaks out of its cocoon, it's time to eat! A female flea can't lay eggs until she has a good meal of blood.

8

FACT BITE

An adult flea will die within a few days if it doesn't find a host and feed.

# The Life Cycle of a Cat Flea

flea eggs

flea larva

flea pupa

flea adult

# BUILT FOR BLOODSUCKING

A flea's mouth is made for sucking blood. It has several parts that all fit together to make a blood-drinking tube fit for a vampire! Two thin, sawlike parts called laciniae (luh-SIH-nee-ee) are used to cut the host's skin. They surround a body part that looks like a needle. Together they're called a stylet.

When a flea bites and the stylet goes through the skin, the flea's mouth and stomach start **pumping**. Blood is sucked through their mouthparts like through a straw!

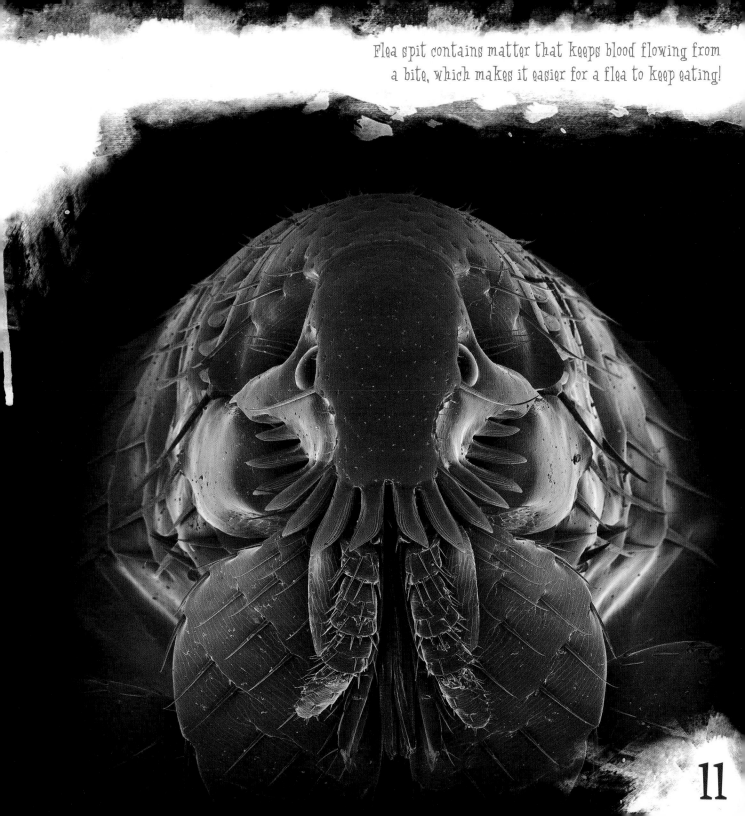

Flea spit contains matter that keeps blood flowing from a bite, which makes it easier for a flea to keep eating!

# BITES AND WORSE

Fleas prefer the blood of dogs and cats over people's blood. Their flat bodies are covered with tiny, gripping hairs that help them crawl through an animal's fur. After they bite, fleas' spit causes **itchy**, painful red bumps on their host's skin.

Many fleas carry tapeworm eggs. The tapeworm is another kind of parasite that hatches and grows inside the flea. If your pet eats a flea with a tapeworm in it, it will get the tapeworm, too!

FACT BITE

Fleas' bodies have a hard outer coating that makes them hard to squish!
It keeps them safe when they're jumping-sometimes from host to host!

13

# TRICKY TICKS

Ticks are another kind of bloodsucking bug! They don't jump or fly, though. They live in shrubs and tall grass, and wait for hosts to walk by so they can crawl on for a meal.

Like fleas, ticks' mouthparts are specially made for sucking blood from a host. A center part looks like a long, **jagged** knife. Two long, hooked parts called chelicerae (kuh-LIH-suh-ree) sit on top of it. These snag the skin and push the knifelike part deep into the poor host.

## FACT BITE

The centre part of a tick's mouth is called the hypostome. It has **barbs** all over it, like a fishhook. When you try to pull a tick off its host, the barbs grab onto the skin even harder!

# LYME DISEASE

Deer ticks are common in the United States. They're known to carry Lyme disease, an illness that can cause heart, eye, and liver problems, and can even cause brain issues. A "bull's-eye" **rash** is the first thing that will tell someone they might have Lyme disease.

Lyme disease can be very serious. The good news is that a tick carrying Lyme disease has to be sucking their host's blood for several hours before passing on the illness.

FACT BITE

Someone with Lyme disease may feel like they have the flu in addition to having a bull's-eye rash like this one. If you have this rash, see a doctor!

# A LIFETIME OF BLOOD

Most kinds of ticks need to drink blood during every part of their life. Because they need so many hosts, it can take years for a tick to finish its life cycle! Many die before they're adults because they can't find enough hosts.

Luckily for ticks, they can feed on warm-blooded animals like people as well as birds, frogs, and lizards. Many ticks like to choose a certain animal to feed on during each part of their life cycle.

**FACT BITE**

Like fleas, ticks have a four-part life cycle: egg, larva, nymph, and adult.

# The Life Cycle
## of a Tick

female
lays
eggs

adult female

adult male

female
larva

male
larva

female nymph

male nymph

19

# BEATING THE BLOODSUCKERS!

The best way to keep from getting sick from tick bites is by checking yourself for ticks right after playing outside in long grass. Check most carefully around your head, neck, and armpits. If you notice a tick on you, have an adult help you pull it off with tweezers!

While fleas do bite people, it's your cats and dogs that need more help! Ask the vet about medicines that can keep fleas away from your pets.

FACT BITE

# WHAT'S BITING YOU?

☑ It sucks blood!

☐ Does it jump?
☐ Is your pet itchy?
☐ Do you have bites on your legs?

## It might be a flea!

☐ Is its body oval?
☐ Do you have bites in a row?
☐ Did you find it in your bed or couch?

## It might be a bedbug!

☐ Is it stuck to you and hard to get off?
☐ Were you in a field or forest today?

## It might be a tick!

☐ Is it in your hair?
☐ Is your head itchy?

## It might be head lice!

# GLOSSARY

**barb:** a sharp point that bends backward and isn't easy to remove

**hatch:** to break open or come out of

**itchy:** having an unpleasant feeling on your skin or inside your mouth or nose that makes you want to scratch

**jagged:** uneven

**organism:** a living thing

**pump:** to force a liquid through a hose or hoselike body part

**rash:** a group of red spots on the skin

**scratch:** to rub one's skin with something to stop an itch

**vampire:** a made-up being who drinks human blood

# FOR MORE INFORMATION

## Books

Hamilton, Robert M. *Ticks*. New York, NY: PowerKids Press, 2016.

Rodger, Ellen. *Bloodsucking Lice and Fleas*. New York, NY: Crabtree Publishing, 2011.

## Websites

**Fun Flea Facts**
*www.health24.com/Lifestyle/Pet-Health/Your-pets-health/Fun-flea-facts-20120721*
Find out more amazing facts about fleas.

**Hey! A Tick Bit Me!**
*kidshealth.org/kid/ill_injure/bugs/tick.html*
Learn more about ticks and how to identify a bite.

**Life Sucks: 10 Amazing Animal Vampires**
*webecoist.momtastic.com/2010/10/05/life-sucks-10-amazing-animal-vampires/*
See photos and find out more about fleas, ticks, and other bloodsuckers.

# INDEX